Buddha Speaks
Messages From
An Ascended Master

Cindy Riggs

©**2016 Cindy Riggs**
All rights reserved.
ISBN: 978-1534636200

No part of this book may be used or reproduced in any manner without prior written permission from the author, except in the case of brief referenced quotations embodied in critical reviews and articles.

Front and back cover photographs taken by and of the author in Nara, Japan.

Acknowledgments

I would like to express my deepest gratitude for the thousands and thousands of spirit beings I have had the honor of channeling as well as the humans who have supported my spiritual work. Along with the Buddha himself, I would like to express a special thanks to Alicia Adams, Amanda Dixon, Caroline Angell, Cathy Kline, Christopher Michaels and Judy Riggs who helped make this book possible.

Introduction

Dear Reader,

Welcome to the perspective of an ascended master! I first encountered The Buddha when I channeled him privately for a client in 2002. I had only been channeling for four years at that point, and exclusively in private sessions. I had primarily channeled spirit guides and nature spirits of Light until that point. The Buddha was my first ascended master, and his energy felt magnificent. I don't have the words he spoke from that first private session, however I have been bestowed with the honor of channeling him regularly ever since.

This book was guided into being by the Buddha himself. It is a compilation of the main themes of which he has spoken through me, and through other aspects of himself, such as Kwan Yin, Avalokitesvara, and Maitreya, transcribed from dozens of recorded group and private channeling sessions over the years.

I am grateful for this opportunity to share his words and energy with you. Words and statements in [brackets] have been added to help facilitate clarification of the concepts presented. Words in bold print are explained in the Glossary. When the Buddha says "we" he is referring to himself as well as those of the higher dimensions in the spirit world. Periodically through this book you will find a brief visualization, exercise or energy transmission, which may be utilized for your meditation that day or for many days, months or years to follow, as you feel guided.

Know that each time you read his words you also receive his compassion and loving energy, which is multi-dimensionally encoded into the words. I trust that you will find the information and energy transmissions as profound and helpful as I have over the years.

May you discover inner peace and alignment with your spiritual path . . . and perhaps even enlightenment!

In Oneness~
Cindy Riggs

Who is The Buddha?

The story of the Buddha's life is one of the most fascinating in human history. Born as Prince Siddhartha Gautama in 623 BCE in southern Nepal, he was carefully sheltered from the world outside the palace and lived a life of luxury. At age 29, his curiosity led him outside where he was exposed to the reality of the harsh life of the common people and began his quest to understand human suffering and find a solution. This began his journey into many different spiritual practices and with different teachers. He was also a student of yoga. When none of these satisfied him, he attempted to find enlightenment through the deprivation of worldly goods including food and nearly starved himself to death.

The most compelling story of his life was at age 35 when he famously meditated under a Pipal (Bodhi) tree in Bodh Gaya, India, where he vowed to remain until he discovered the truth. It was said that he meditated for 49 days until he achieved his awakening, in which he gained clear insight into the cause of suffering and the steps necessary to eliminate it.

For the remainder of his life, known as the Buddha (enlightened one) he traveled and taught his Four Noble Truths (through which a state of liberation is said to be possible for any being), The Noble Eightfold Path of Liberation (principles that everyone can use to achieve enlightenment) and The Middle Way, a path of moderation between the extremes of self-indulgence and self-mortification.

The Four Noble Truths

1. The Truth of Suffering: all conditional experiences are not ultimately satisfying; suffering is a fact of life.
2. The Truth of the Cause of Suffering: craving for and clinging to what is pleasurable, and aversion to what is not pleasurable.
3. The Truth of the End of Suffering: putting an end to craving and clinging.
4. The Truth of the Noble Eightfold Path of Liberation: by behaving with pure understanding, attitude, speech, action, livelihood, effort, mindfulness and concentration, an end can be put to craving, to clinging, to becoming, to dissatisfaction, and to the cycle of death and rebirth.

The Noble Eightfold Path of Liberation

1. Right Understanding - to understand the Law of Cause and Effect and the Four Noble Truths.
2. Right Attitude - not harboring thoughts of greed and anger.
3. Right Speech - avoid lying, gossip, harsh speech and tale telling.
4. Right Action - not to destroy any life, not to steal or commit adultery.
5. Right Livelihood - avoiding occupations that bring harm to oneself and others.
6. Right Effort - earnestly doing one's best in the right direction.
7. Right Mindfulness - always being aware and attentive.
8. Right Concentration - making the mind steady and calm in order to realize the true nature of things.

Contents

Illusion 1

Reality 3

Duality 9

Divine Order 14
   Energy Transmission 19

Perception 20

Compassion 21

Peace 22
   Meditation To Create Space for Peace 25

Presence 26

Time 29

Still Silence 32
   Presence Meditation 33

Allowing 33

Alignment 36
   Alignment Exercise 42

Grounding 42

Manifesting Reality 43

The Source of Guidance 45

Cycles 47

Your Purpose	50
You Are Contributing to Evolution	53
Golden Light Visualization	*54*
Healing	55
Letting Go *Is* Healing	56
Healing Energy Transmission	*58*
Buddha Nature/Enlightenment	59
The Lotus Blooms	64
Illumination	65
Illumination Initiation	*72*
Glossary	75
About The Author	83

Buddha Speaks
Messages From
An Ascended Master

Cindy Riggs

Illusion

I am **Siddhartha**. Blessings to you, my brothers and sisters. Thank you for sharing this space with me.

I wish to speak to you about illusion. Think about what the definition of illusion is to you. Something unseen? Something untrue, perhaps? What is illusion? My answer may differ from yours, and yours will differ from the person next to you and so on. The important message is that your surroundings, your atmosphere, your environment—it is illusion . . . and it is also *not* illusion. Things are as real as you believe they are. Perhaps you have heard this before—nothing new.

Think about what you believe about everything that you see, or taste, or touch, or smell, or sense. Those of you who have developed your consciousness beyond the **3rd dimension** may either be confused or unsure because the things that you see, or sense, or hear, or know, you cannot prove. Yet there are many things in your nature that you cannot prove or understand completely. So my message to you is to open your mind to the fact that your environment—your immediate environment—or the things that you can see outside the window . . . perhaps they are not really there . . . or perhaps they are really there, and there is so much more that you are unable to see because you do not *believe* it is there.

Each day I would encourage you to open your mind to the fact that what is in your view may not be the entire picture. See if you can see beyond the 3rd dimension with your eyes. See if you can hear beyond the 3rd dimension with your ears. I will tell you that you can. But humans tend to not believe they can, until they see it or hear it. But I will tell you that you must believe it first, and then you will see it, and then you will hear it.

So you have heard that all of your life is illusion, that matter is only illusion and that it truly does not *matter*. This is true and this is not true. It depends on from where you are viewing that reality. If, from where you are viewing it, it *matters*, then it is matter. I would like to encourage you to view it from space perhaps, from another place, from another place of awareness where you already have in your thinking mind, your consciousness, the fact or the concept that it may be simply illusion.

You notice how I said "fact" did you not? Illusion defined for you usually means it is not real, but what is real? Just because you hold it in your hand you think that it is real, and yet when you're having a dream and you are holding something in your hand it is real, and then when you wake from the dream it seems that that was not real, and yet it was while you were in the dream. My message to you is to remind you that you are in the dream here. You are in an ongoing dream, one that has dreams embedded in it while you are sleeping. What a fascinating multi-dimensional creature you are to have this capability. Are dreams silly? Are they meaningless? No. They're simply just another reality which seems silly once you awake, doesn't it sometimes? It made perfect sense while you were there, and then as soon as you wake it makes no sense at all. How can this be? This is the nature of reality. Different planes of existence, parallel Universes, different worlds. All real—and all illusion. And all for a **purpose**—a **Divine** purpose.

You are all seeking more wisdom, more knowledge, more [spiritual] experiences like this. So believe that you will have them, and as you do, you will have more of them. And the more you have, the more you will believe . . . and so the more you will have.

This can be complicated when it is being explained only with words. Obviously, an experience is necessary. What is imagination . . . when you say something was "just your imagination?" What is that? What is that thing? It must be energy, because thoughts are energy. So, from where does it come? Perhaps this is what I am speaking about. Illusion . . . or reality. Perhaps illusion is simply a word that describes that which you cannot explain. Does that mean it is not real? It does not. So I encourage you to pay attention to dreams, and to things that you believe you are making up in your mind. Or when you think your eyes "play tricks on you", which does not make scientific sense. If you *think* you saw something, perhaps you did. But you will not begin to see it until you believe you did.

Reality

Summer solstice is a very powerful time for manifestation, for major shifts within your being: physically, mentally and emotionally for a giant leap forward in your spiritual evolution. Oh, you've heard this before. Isn't it always an "auspicious" time? Perhaps. I would say that there is no time like the present to work on your spiritual evolution, and we can say that at any moment, but there are some powerful cycles happening on your planet . . . not just on your planet but on the multi-dimensions of where you believe you exist in this hologram. Major shifts occurring which feel very real, which feel very concrete, which seem to *matter*.

You are receiving more energy from the sun every day, today, tomorrow, the next day; more and more energy coming to you. Do you still feel tired and exhausted? If so, you're not utilizing this source of free energy that is being presented each day. This doesn't mean you lie in the sun, necessarily. You look out your window and you allow its rays to permeate your being.

I will summarize . . . solstice, one of high energy. This is when you put out your solar panel and soak it all up (not literally) and store some for later. But if you do not, then I must remind you that you have access to unlimited energy at any time, not only from your planet's core but from your heart center. That access point deep within your heart that is directly connected to **Source** Itself. If you think of these things every day then you would not need to play in the sun, but I would encourage you to do so anyway because it's fun and it's healing on many levels. Allow it to soak into all of your cells, energizing them. It's not about darkening your skin, it's about energizing your batteries. It's a recharger for your batteries. Every cell in your body is like a battery—every subatomic particle.

Naturally humans want to spend more time outside or at least awake when there is more sun. Your batteries are charged. What do you do with this energy then? So much energy…is it too much? Then share it with others. Then channel it down into the Earth. You want to help your Earth so much, along with [recycling] your paper or your cans.

Send some energy into your planet. But not if you are drained, you need to pull energy up from the planet. And it is more than willing to [recharge you] if you simply ask.

What is causing your batteries to drain? Nothing drains your batteries faster than negative thinking, worry, fear, apprehension, lack of self-confidence, guilt, frustration, depression, anxiety; nothing drains you faster than these concepts which cause emotion. These emotions require a lot of fuel. This is how you become drained—not so much your physical workout, not even so much your mental thought patterns around your work each day. It is the negative thought which for many humans is automatic, is running on autopilot now . . . the human not even aware that they are choosing these thoughts in each moment. Do not be a victim to your illusion of reality. Be a leader. Be the leader of your reality. Nothing happens that can truly harm you. Nothing happens here that is truly damaging to your **Soul** unless you judge it to be. Someone harms you or someone murders you, you're not damaged unless you decide to build a framework around the concept of . . . some type of victim concept. Not necessary, and very, very draining.

What humans need to remember while they're learning *how* to re-member [with their True Selves] is that all is energy: the body is energy, thoughts are energy. And the thoughts . . . all of this rampant thinking, all of this over-thinking and over-analyzing is draining the body of energy. You have only so much energy each day that you carry around with you that can fuel your thoughts, your emotions and your tasks/your physical body. And when you are depleted, this starts to take a toll on the health and well being of the physical body. So understand that you only have so much in your "account" so to speak each day, and if you do not replenish this, over time you begin to have a number of different issues, such as nervous disorders, or cancer or other **dis-ease**, or even colds and flu. These types of things are all a result of draining your Self of energy from all of this thinking.

[Audience Question] What else can we do to feed our bodies with the correct food? Exercise?

[Buddha] First of all, each person is unique, and so the one who discovered one particular method of eating has discovered the one that is correct for them—and perhaps has helped many other people too. But it is important for the individual to listen to the [their own] body. Now, this part is difficult because the body has a tendency to crave what it is given, such as sugar, such as drugs, alcohol; and so it is important to understand that no human body wants chemicals or toxins inside of it. And so, when one says, "Well, I am craving sugar, my body must need sugar." Mmmm . . . some sugar is fine, such as natural sugar from fruit, but the sugar that is processed . . . anything that is out of its natural state is not going to be harmonious with the body. So the more raw food that can be ingested and the purest water, and the purest whole food supplements, these types of things everyone knows are good for them . . . and yet many other things are called food and it is up to the individual to find the plan that works best for them. There are many, many other humans that are willing to help with this.

Muscle-testing is one of the most accurate methods for determining the diet and the supplementation, as well as the energy. The energy is more important in fact, because when the body has enough energy to function properly, then it is not in a state of inflammation as often. So it is both: first you need the purest food, or food in the state that holds the purest energy/the highest amount of energy. So you can imagine that spinach picked from the ground and eaten immediately has the most energy/the most life force contained within it. Once it is shipped, packaged, and then cooked, it has lost much of its life force. And so the closer you can get to its life force, the better for the body. But as important as that is, the mental and emotional energetic state must be replenished as well. And sleeping is not enough for most humans.

"That which is occurring is just occurring."

Now, many humans are existing in a state of fight-or-flight all of the time—you call this "anxiety." And this state of being is draining you of so much energy. And some humans in this state then begin to feed off other humans for energy and they create drama so they can pull others into this drama so they can feed off the energy. Usually it is a negative type of energy because this is the only way you can "steal" from others, so to speak.

Taking a look at the planet . . . lots going on? Lots always going on. Know that everything that is occurring is not "new." Nothing is ever new. You can label it as new. You can decide that it's new because you have not experienced it before, but nothing is new. Technology is new, perhaps; but the issues, the fears, the tragedies, the crimes—none of them are new. Don't be so surprised, this is all I'm saying. Don't be so surprised. In fact, it is most helpful if you look at that which is occurring which you would call "negative" and just decide that, well, because it is not new and because it is just happening, it just *is*, and that is that.

Can you imagine how [life will be], if you will free your Self, when you do not judge things as "negative" or "wrong" or "bad" or "tragedy?" Because even those concepts in your mind create negative force flowing through you, create negative emotion. Negative emotion then, within your law of attraction concept, attracts negative experience, yes? Negative thought creates negative emotion creates negative experience. And so you are doing it to your Self. And then you become frustrated. With whom are you frustrated? Your Self? And then you beat your Self up, and then you damage your **solar plexus chakra**, and then you drain your energy and then you are in a vicious circle, or cycle of negativity. See? Only you can bring your Self out of it.

I will inspire you . . . hopefully help you to rise above some of the pettiness of the 3rd dimensional space. I am calling it "pettiness" because deep down you know that it is petty. Deep down you know that it does not matter. What matters is nothing, because nothing is matter. And yet the definition you have for "matter" is: [that which is] important. And isn't this interesting that you use a word that describes that which is solid—or "real" as you call it—also as something that is very important. Fascinating that this one term describes both of these concepts. Nothing is matter. All is energy vibrating at different frequencies, different densities.

Hopefully you have noticed some synchronicities, some things that have occurred quite effortlessly for you today. Think of at least one thing that has, and that will lead to more things in your awareness, and that will create more in your reality.

Duality

You are born in a perfect state, free of **duality** for awhile, yet trapped in a very small container. You come in pure and clear. Although some come in with some **karma**, this is not remembered. Some come and bring energy from **past lives** with them—most of you do—but this is not consciously remembered by most, not in the beginning . . . although this is becoming more of an awareness in children as you have heard of now—over the past twenty years primarily—children who have access to the remembrance of past lives and of other planes of existence.

So you come in here pretty clear and pure and then you begin to experience the duality, which I will call **contrast**. This plane of existence that includes the energy charges of "negative" and "positive." **Yin** and **Yang**/feminine and masculine are not negative and positive; these are *aspects* of both negative *and* positive. Yin and Yang representing the feminine and masculine; and *then* [duality represents] the positive and the negative. So it is almost like a cross. Your feminine side is your left side of the body; your masculine is the right side of the body. Duality happening in the entire body: good and bad, right and wrong, **Love** and fear. And the *mind* engages in the duality of right and wrong, good and bad. The Soul always remembers the purity of no duality—the purity of pure **Light** and Love.

Love is the purest form of **Creative Force**. Light is the masculine aspect, Love the Feminine; but ultimately it all comes from Love, pure Source.

A lot going on already, yes? So then you start experiencing your life collecting memories, collecting experiences. Some of them you call positive, some of them you call negative. And yet, even in the space of duality where both charges exist, most of your experiences, whether positive or negative, are perceptions of your mind, because the mind understands only positive or negative, right or wrong, good or bad. And so it wants to categorize the experience as a good one or a bad one. Only two ways that you can think: positively or negatively. And every time you think, you are *choosing* to think either positively or negatively.

And then learned behaviors collect within your mind and they become automatic, because the mind has that ability. Two ways you can think, [but] three ways you can *be*: positive or negative or *neutral*. Being in the present moment in your heart center, centered and aligned, you have a third choice of *being*. And in the state of being/the state of meditation or deep trance is the state in which you can have access to **All That Is**: wisdom, knowledge, **guidance**. It is that state that most are trying to attain if you are interested in enlightenment, interested in increased spiritual awareness. It is that *being* state—that third choice—that is most powerful, that has the most direct access to Source. In the heart center where your Soul is anchored, so to speak.

You are a point of Light experiencing a human form in a space of duality. Very, very challenging. Very courageous for anyone who incarnates here. Give your Self credit for this. Beating your Self up also takes place in this region [solar plexus], and that, of course, is self-defeating, holding you back.

Some humans say, "Why do I not have the psychic awareness that I seek?" It is not that the psychic awareness is not available to you; it is that you are holding your Self back in some way. Usually it is that you believe it is not possible for you, you believe that you are not good enough, believe that you're not qualified. And yet, everyone has this ability. Everyone has the ability of insight. It is natural. It is a part of your *being* as you come in here. It was never meant to be disconnected, so *know* that. Know that it is there, and know that . . . it is not that you "deserve" it, it is an entitlement for being the point of Light that you are.

Humans also say, "Well, I have a dark side and I'm afraid of that dark side." And they go for hypnosis or some other technique . . . or they are even afraid of the psychic/discovering of the dark side. And yet everyone has it. One human said to this one [Cindy] that they felt as though they could murder someone, and they were surprised that they had that within them. And yet, this is within everyone here in duality. But you work to rise above that, yes? Every day you work to rise above the dual part of your Self or the shadow part of your Self. It is there. It is meant to be there. That is part of this experience. But inner peace is achievable. "Inner peace" is a label, sure, but for you it is a feeling, perhaps here [solar plexus], perhaps here [heart center], perhaps everywhere.

This is a free will zone. Free will choice of thought. Everything stems from thought. The physical body responds to thought, the mental body, the emotional bodies respond to thought. You cannot even experience an emotion, wherever you experience it, unless you have had a thought.

You cannot feel sad unless you have had a thought or a judgment that it is a sad situation. You do not have to choose to feel sad. You do not have to choose to feel happy. But realize that you are choosing. If you're feeling guilty about something that happened in the past, you can choose to let go of it in this moment. Or you can continue to choose to keep it alive in your mind every day *with a pattern of habit of thought*.

And yes, this can become dis-ease, this can become chemical imbalance, and these things must be treated because they have gotten too far out of control. Some of you are born into that, but that is still not the excuse for not changing it. Is it hard work? Only if you believe it is. Whatever you choose to believe is true. I lived this. I know this. I understand. I was a teacher. I lived it so I could teach it. Many of you are experiencing things so you can teach them to others later on, or write about them, or say things about them, or whatever it is you choose to do here that you *feel* is your fullest expression of your Self—your **True Self**. If you do not know what your True Self is, entertain the concept that there is a True Self. Where does it live? You determine. Because the truth is that it lives in every particle of your being: always there, always sparkling, always perfect Light.

So you come here to try something else—a different body, a different set of parents, a different situation, different karmas to play out. And we in the **spirit** world hear all the time: "How can I erase my karma?", "I wish to not have to experience karma." What if karma is not something negative? Why must it always be negative, this concept of karma? Karma is something that plays out regardless of your awareness of it. In fact many of you played out some karma just today. Not very painful, was it? It's not always dramatic. Only your mind wants to think that things must be dramatic—your dual mind, your ego mind. And yet, what motivates you to **evolve**, to change? Usually it's contrast. Usually it's something you would label as unpleasant that motivates you to feel more pleasant, to be in a situation that feels more pleasant or positive. It is important that you have these labels. I do not wish you to erase them all. But my message is that I suggest that you notice when your labels or your judgments are negative, and see if you can shift them into something that are their opposite.

You have some things happening with your politics, your healthcare happening here. Many are opposed. Many are resisting what is occurring. Leaders are making decisions that many people do not agree with. Why would this occur? Why would a leader make a decision that the general population does not agree with? There's a reason for that. Because there is something positive that will come out of it. It *seems* to be contrast, it *appears* to be contrast, perhaps you are *perceiving* it as contrast—choosing to as a collective or as an individual—and yet, it just *is*. It is a decision that was made by a leader. Why would you think that your leader is incapable of making the decision that is appropriate for the evolution of the human species? Because something comes into being that is new or never done before. Why is this always wrong? Why is this always met with resistance?

I will explain why. Because your mind only knows what it has been programmed from the past. And if something new is introduced: a new plan, a new project, a new configuration of energy; you have no frame of reference for this new organization of energy, and therefore it takes some effort for you to choose to accept and allow it to manifest, or play out, as it is meant to. Leaders are leaders for a reason, because they have more access to information. They have become your leaders for a reason.

Divine Order

Everything is in **Divine Order**, and everything is happening as it is meant to happen for the benefit of humanity, even though it does not seem to appear that way much of the time. Many people are killed through a natural disaster. Many people are killed through some kind of airplane crash or other event that happens on Earth's surface. People are killed through dis-ease. And you think this is "tragedy." If you realize that you simply recycle your Selves, is not a tragedy at all. Perhaps "getting out of class early" is a good thing, "getting released from work early" is freedom—freedom to choose something different the next time. You are living in illusion. You are living in a hologram. For you to become attached to anyone or anything, you are attaching your Self to *concept*, to illusion.

Know that your world is exactly how it is meant to be. Do not be angry with your politicians. Do not be angry with your structures or your organizations. Do not fear for Earth's resources. Everything will work itself out for the greatest benefit of the collective human evolution. Trust that. *Know* that. When you know that—or at least when you believe it—you free your Self from the negative, fearful-based broadcast that has been occurring in your mind.

Do not worry about what your governments are up to. Simply send Love to those organizations, and you are done, you are complete. When you send Love to something or someone, there is nothing to intend, there is nothing to try to fix or heal. You present Love, as I present it to you. And then it is utilized in the way that either the person accepts it or doesn't; the organization notices it or doesn't. Love is the most powerful "weapon" so to speak. You're angry at a person? You will never become enlightened if you remain angry, or feel guilt; it is not possible. All of those things need to be erased bit-by-bit, every single day as you notice your thoughts. That is all you have to do. Be present and notice how you are choosing to think. The way you feel tells you how you are choosing to think. Your reality/your environment shows you how you are choosing to think. And if you do not like what you see or do not like what you feel, choose differently. It's that simple.

So many organizations fighting against that which is undesirable, whether it is disease or famine, whether it is agreed-upon rules, whether it is even what is right and wrong to eat. Fighting against . . . what have your wars taught you? Fighting is effective in what? The illusion of control? If you understood how thoughts broadcast energy, and if you understood that your worry and your concern over something is actually broadcasting negative energy toward that person or thing that you are worried about, you would never worry, because you do not want to harm that person, you do not wish to harm your own future. Why would you pollute or populate your own future with negative energy? Why would you do that? This is like blowing toxic smoke into the room where you are about to sleep. Why would you do that to your Self? Why would you worry about something that has not happened—and may never happen? Why would you be attached to something that has the potential to be greater than you can imagine? Why would you be attached to an object or a person when it's simply just energy **particles**?

But this is "big picture" speak, and I plant it in your mind for a reason, because you already know it—you know it to be true—and you will integrate this information in the time that is appropriate for you. And as you integrate the information you affect the human collective in a way that is evolutionary. So perhaps you are wondering if this information will "help" humanity. So many humans say, "I wish to help.", "I wish to serve humanity." You cannot serve humanity by *doing* as much as you can serve humanity by *being*. If you are in a state of Love—pure Love—you are affecting the human collective more efficiently and effectively than any donation of time or money by starting with the one you see reflected in the mirror. This is how you serve humanity – you inspire others with your state of *being*. The doing comes easily. You do not have to think about what to do, what is appropriate to do, what is the thing you are "supposed" to do. For most humans there is no "supposed to." What if this is true? I'm telling you that it is.

You are told that "all things are possible." You are also told that "no one is perfect." If all things are possible and yet it is impossible to be perfect, then how do you set your goals? This is confusing information. You are told that "practice makes perfect." But you are also told that you cannot be perfect. Your society is fascinating, and it is based in duality—just as you are, just as I was. I experienced lavish royalty as well as poverty. I wanted to understand it all. Extremes of contrast led me to balance.

I encourage you to think more about reality as the truth of that which it is: it is particles, energy particles. I want you to think of everything simply as particles displaying themselves in a certain pattern in each moment. Each moment is different. Each person's body changes from moment to moment in its balance and its particle configuration. Anything can be shifted much quicker than most humans believe. And suffering is the result of forgetting that a human is simply a particle configuration, and those particles are made of Love/Light of Creative Force. And so it is important to ignore issues or situations in which there is no material evidence in the moment.

Evidence is most important—not what you call "hearsay"—and yet still I can see it in your minds: thoughts are entertained in which there is still no information [evidence] yet. And this is a waste of your energy and it removes you from the present, which is the only time that you have, the only true reality . . . and yet, the truth is that you are eternal and so expansive that you can't even conceive of it in your mind. So the phrase you have "this too shall pass" is very, very important to understand because most things do pass away, except for in the mind. The reality is no longer there, only a hologram in the mind of what was. But you are in the hologram now of what *is*. And it is from the present moment that you can create or manifest the most powerful outcomes. Not by being attached to a specific outcome, but by being . . . present.

You are not here for bliss all of the time. And if you are, you no longer need to be here, which will be fine for you, if you achieve it. If you are here to experience the poverty or the contrast . . . not necessarily poverty—do not be alarmed! I realize money is a touchy subject with many humans and it need not be. It is created from Love, just like everything else—you allow it into your field just as you allow a partner or a career or any other opportunities, friendships, **synchronicities**. Do not fear that which is part of you: particles of Love.

"Whatever you fear, you push away from your Self."

Money is just energy. So money is no different than a friend, money is no different than an opportunity, money is no different than a guided message, money is no different than a physical body, or a chair or carpet.

Whatever you fear, you push away from your Self. And whatever you fear, you begin to label as something negative. All negative thoughts are rooted in fear. Do you realize this? Many humans will say, "I am not fearful, I am not scared." And yet guilt is fear, anxiety is fear—usually fear in which you cannot control the outcome/you do not have the power to control. You have the power to control a great deal with your choices of perception, your choices of thought. I am presenting this to you because it is very, very important for you to understand and begin to practice so that you can see your reality changing, you can see your world becoming brighter. If you'll simply choose to put on those "rose-colored glasses" as you call them, rather than the dark ones.

How do you choose to see your reality? How do you choose to perceive other people? You cannot change them. You cannot control the carpet or the chair, but you can decide if a chair is beautiful or if it is ugly. Each of you has a different perception of the look of a chair, how it appears to you. Does it look soft, rough, comfortable, pretty? Does it look well-designed, well-built? Does it look cheap? And how do you determine those things? And why do you determine those things? Because you think it matters, because you call it "matter." And *it matters* . . . as long as you *think* it matters. Humans will always say, "Well, this is going to be very hard.", "This is going to be difficult.", "I don't know how to do this." And I have already explained it: you just [choose to] do it. You just *be* it.

***

Energy Transmission

Sit comfortably, relax and take a few deep breaths, then proceed to read Buddha's words, which are embedded with powerful energy frequencies for you:

I transmit golden fibers of Light to you now, penetrating wherever energy deficits exist within your whole being, so if you are feeling energy now in a particular area of your body this is where there is a deficit . . . or perhaps just an easy door to penetrate your fields. Just helping you to reenergize, fix that which is weak or weakened by negative thinking. Allow it to assist you, allow it to permeate your being.
***

Perception

"…When it comes to spiritual growth you cannot have evidence first. You must believe and then the evidence will show itself. It depends on from where you are perceiving reality."

I want to speak of perception: the most important concept you can understand. From where are you perceiving your reality? Just with the tasting, touching and the smelling and the seeing and the hearing? What about the *knowing*? It's the sense you were born with. The one that could be stronger than all the others, the one that hears guidance from other places—from the inner consciousness or the unconscious mind. Many labels for this: **Higher Self**, **guidance system**, **guidance team**, **spirit guides**. All of you are surrounded with teams of different spirits assisting you.

And there is this concept that humans have that there is some spirit outside of them that is judging them in the same manner. This is never true. Not I or anyone else in the spirit world is judging you. Only you. And yet you are led to believe that that is true. Unless you have evidence that this is true, why would you believe so? And yet, when it comes to spiritual growth you cannot have evidence first. You must believe and then the evidence will show itself. It depends on from where you are perceiving reality. If you are perceiving it from the 3rd dimension, then matter does *matter*. If you are perceiving it from above or outside of the 3rd and **4th dimensions**, then you realize that everything just *is*.

Compassion

I come to deliver a message about **compassion**. When there is a person or persons who are causing you some disruption, some confusion—perhaps frustration or even fear—see if you can jump to compassion first. See if you can understand they are operating from fear, if they are behaving in a negative manner. See if you can . . . not *understand* them, but *accept* that there is fear involved. When you acknowledge this fear or when you are in the state of being of acceptance, you create space for them to grow, you create space for them to expand, and you release all resistance. Do not jump to conclusions, jump to compassion.

Relationships need not be a power struggle, but understanding is helpful. Understanding is not always possible. Even entertaining the idea of understanding is helpful. And all you need to understand is that the other may be operating from fear, if the situation is in conflict. This is where I learned compassion. For some will never understand and some will never "change" as you say. But the compassion holds the space for—creates the space for—their own awakening, their own understanding, their own growth.

Remember that each person has a different filter with which they perceive reality. Sometimes it is fun and helpful to entertain the concepts or ideas of those other perceptions, those other filters. Choose compassion for those who are operating through the filter of fear or insignificance. Notice when you are operating from fear. And even confusion is rooted in fear. I would encourage you to ponder and even ask for the Self-Love that will align the one that has cast you away. I am Buddha. I teach compassion. And so, no one in human form ever exhibits traits of negativity or fear unless there is fear inside, or insecurity. So wish for those types of people Self-Love, Self-realization. That is all that is necessary.

Peace

"You cannot force things into being and be in a state of peace."

I wish to talk with you briefly about peace, because peace will not occur in your world. Do not look for it in your world; look for it in your Self. Where is peace found? Within. Always within. Why? What is peace? There is a different definition of peace within each one of your minds. Each one of your concepts is different. And yet it is usually understood to be calmness, tranquility, centeredness, alignment.

Do not wait for peace to happen outside of you. "Peace" is a concept anyway. And yet you each have your own definition of peace. No two definitions exactly alike. Peace will not happen around you first. You create peace. You can be the prince or princess of peace by broadcasting it, by choosing it. No matter what is happening, you choose peace. You choose to not label it. You choose to not engage in negative thought or negative conversation. Remember that as long as you are here in duality there will not be peace. There is not supposed to be peace. Duality is the opposite of peace. To know peace is to know contrast here in this space. So when you do experience contrast, express gratitude for it. In fact, express gratitude for everything you can think of in your life. Make a list. Make a gratitude list. Not just on your Thanksgiving holiday. Gratitude for all that you are and all that you have, knowing *what* you are, *knowing that you know* the truth, which is that you are a point of Light, an aspect of Source/Creator/God.

Do not look for peace. Re-discover it, re-member with it, remember that it is there. You are a pure, clear Light at your core. You are pure Love. Everything else is illusion: the body is illusion, the mind is illusion, every thought you have ever had in this lifetime and in other lifetimes is illusion.

I would encourage you to think also of peace throughout your holiday season as you are caught up in stresses and family issues and all of this unnecessary shopping that takes place. In every task, in every day, every moment, ask your Self, "Is this bringing me peace?" If it is bringing you stress then how is it helping you or others? Do not be stressed to share gifts with others; but does it bring you peace? Are you doing it gracefully? Are you handling situations gracefully, peacefully, with presence of mind? So much is spoken about "presents" this time of year: boxes with bows, bags with tissue. What about the most important *present*: this moment? Your *presence*. Your choice of having your mind in the now . . . probably the most powerful technique you could use for enlightenment. So peace . . . always asking your Self, "Does this bring me peace?"

[Question from a radio talk show host] "How do we bring more peace into our world when so many political leaders of different countries are war-mongering . . . ?"

[Buddha] To bring more peace into the life space . . . first of all *the space has to be made* for peace to occur. So if people are running around in their "Type A" state of being—or their anxious state of being—there is no time [or space] for peace. And yet they keep searching for it, they keep asking for it, they keep praying for it. But how will they expect it to occur if they will not slow down and be still? One must be still and silent. I have heard humans say, "Well, jogging is my meditation." or "Gardening is my meditation." That is not being still. Yes, that is a type of meditation . . . it is a brainwave state where one is more focused or a little more relaxed; but one must be still and silent to create the space for peace. Peace cannot come without the space.

How can you expect to have the clean **aura**, or a clean energy field, when you are not stopping to clean it? So, space must be made for peace, and then peace can occur. How to find peace? One must be present. For the mind to spend time in the past or the future, it only creates anxiety because the future and the past do not actually exist. Only the present exists and only in the present can the space be made for peace, and then in that space you can now begin to manifest your desires.

Some kind of exercise movement is helpful. Each person knows what is appropriate for them. Some love to run, some love yoga, some just simply need to stretch. Remember that stretching the physical body actually helps to promote more flow of energy through the **meridians**. So even stretching is helpful. Body, mind and spirit—all three [receiving] equal attention. The body: you take care of the body with food and exercise. The mind: you quiet the mind

and think more positively. And the spirit: make space for peace.
***

Meditation To Create Space for Peace

Sit comfortably, relax and take a few deep breaths. The following meditation may be practiced indefinitely. Intend to receive the energy from Buddha each time you practice.

Close your eyes for moment, and imagine the chakra or vortex spinning in the heart center and that it is the color green. Open up that heart center like you are opening up a portal. I am sending a golden frequency of Light—allow it to come into your heart. Breathe in and allow this energy to come into your heart, populate your body; and once it populates your entire body, allow it to extend outside the body into your auric field.
***

As this is occurring, I just want to remind: the more that you let go of the mind, the more you let go of understanding and allow the experience to happen in your heart center, the more clarity you will receive, the more intuition you will receive, the more guidance you will understand. And yet it is not understanding in the mind. It is a knowing. Knowing occurs in the center of the body in the heart, and in the solar plexus, and in the navel. Knowing does not occur in the mind. Knowledge is one thing, knowing is another. Knowledge is information or data that you have collected throughout your lifetime and it is stored in your brain. Knowing is that which you feel to be true. Knowing is that feeling of you, the Divine. Know that you already know everything you could ever need to know. And you access that from the center of your energy system—from your navel to your heart—that whole center is your receiving center, so receive others' energy there, receive information there, receive this golden Light there now.

Presence

"Please be as present as you can be. For then you will receive the greatest benefit."

I am the one you call The Buddha, Siddhartha. Thank you for allowing me to join you, beautiful Lights. I hope that you can think of your Selves as beautiful Lights, because this is what you are. However, I am seeing a great deal of anxiety. That's why I have come. I come to bring calm presence and to help you to understand how to generate within your Self, *calm presence*.

Presence is where you know that all is well and you are completely present. That is the state of *being* to strive for, and yet it is not expected for you to remain there all the time. Once you remain there for an extended period of time, it is no longer necessary for you to be here [incarnate], because there are no more lessons to learn and no more motivation for you. You have eternity to experience that state of being. But it is wonderful when you can transcend duality and experience that once in a while, while you are here, yes? And you have all experienced it at some point, even if it was just for a moment.

So relax into your *now*. Some humans, when they understand the concept of *presence* or *now*, they think about it too much. And what they do not understand is that it is a state of *being*, not a state of thinking. And while it may be impossible for you to quiet your thoughts—next to impossible, yes, for most—it is achievable. And even if just for a moment, or a split-second, it is propelling you forward so quickly in your spiritual evolution. And that is the purpose that you are here: your spiritual evolution.

Remember this: once you have experienced something, you can experience it again. Does this mean that once you have experienced something unpleasant, you can experience it again? Of course. You can also experience something pleasant. I hear humans all of the time saying, "It is deeply ingrained.", "It has been like this since I was small.", "My parents have taught me this and therefore, this is how I believe or how I must be.", "My astrology chart is a certain way, and this is how I must act or operate." These are all sources of blame for not taking responsibility for presence—being present and changing the one thing that you can change: you, your personality, your behavior. The *one* thing that you *can* control is the one thing where everything begins: your thoughts/your choices of thought. Every thought is a choice and if you do not think that is true, then you are not present.

So, something happens like an earthquake or a tsunami. What is this? What is this occurrence to you? Each one of your minds thinks about it differently, perceives it differently. How do you hear about the event? Do you hear it on your news media? Do you hear about it from a friend? Do you read about it in your newspaper? And as you hear or see about this event—whether you are reading it or hearing about it or both at the same time—what happens immediately? The mind goes to work because it is magnificent, and it decides in an instant whether that event was good or bad. What if you were present—completely present, not thinking—and you obtained this information? Have you ever done this? Have you ever experienced this detached emotion where you receive the information and all of a sudden it is known that it is neither good nor bad, it is neither right nor wrong, it is neither tragedy nor . . . whatever you determine the opposite of tragedy to be? What if it just is something that occurred?

See if you can practice *being* more than ever before. See if you can practice presence . . . and hesitation. Wait until you respond. Wait until you answer a question. Give your Self a moment to *know that you know* how to speak, what to say, how to act. And the space between words, the space between action is the most powerful space where connections are made.

[Client question] "Being present in the moment and seeing the reality in front of me—being realistic, right?"

[Buddha] Being realistic in that the present reality is the only one. And yet you must think about the future. But think about the future from a place of *presence*. Think about your desires, but do not be attached to the future outcome. Because if you are not attached to the future outcome, but are attached to something more magnificent that you can't [yet] imagine, then you create even more space for the more magnificent possibility to show itself.

I will attempt to say it another way: in that you revel in the present thinking with excitement and with positive emotion about the goal or the objective, and you stay only with that. You don't start looking for it to occur. It is as though you are "keeping the fire burning." Because a fire is very *present*. You must keep adding wood to the fire. So each day you are adding wood to the fire by saying, "I want this present fire to remain burning brightly and all I have to do is add something to it right now, so that it continues to burn in the future." But you do not know how high it will burn. You do not know in what patterns it will burn. You just know that you can keep nurturing it, keep nurturing the goal or desire.

Time

"If you are truly present, you can slow down time."

Time. I wish for you to think about time in this manner as well. And yet if you are truly present—which takes some practice (I will admit it took me a lot of practice) —you can slow down time, maybe even stop it. But this concept of time is different for everyone as well. Humans will say, "This will take me a long time to figure out.", "This will take me a long time to heal or a long time to let go of." What is a long time? For some, two minutes is a long time. Ask a child how long two minutes is. For others, two hours is a long time. For another, two years may be a long time. None of this [concept of time] is tangible, with the ability to actually quantify it. You have your clocks and all of your other devices keeping time, and yet what is your perception of time? Does it take a long time to get to work? This one [Cindy] had an awareness when she was on a long flight, when she was beginning to entertain the ideas of being/presence and of perception. The flight was scheduled for twelve hours overseas from where she lives. And as she was sitting on the plane, she realized it was not a *long* flight, it was simply a flight she was on. And that awareness has helped her tremendously, not just about time, but about other events as well.

It is important to understand that your perception or your awareness must keep up with the times. It must keep up with the quickening that is occurring here. Some will say, "Time isn't actually moving faster, it is just that you are perceiving it as faster." That is partly true. The other part is that it is indeed moving faster. This is what happens when **frequency** changes. But each person is perceiving it differently. Those operating at a lower frequency will continue to perceive reality moving at the same pace as always. Those moving up in frequency will perceive it as faster only because they are not 100% present. When you are completely aligned and present you will notice that time slows, you can almost even stop time in the *presence of being*. Practice this. The more you practice *presence*, the more you will receive all that you desire, and hopefully more than you can imagine: awareness, messages, synchronicities . . . enlightenment even.

"What do you believe you can and cannot do? I suspect that what you believe you cannot do is illusion. That is not the truth. Because the truth is that you are capable of anything—anything you desire. A mind as vast as the Universe with access to all the power—more power than you can imagine. But you must believe first. Be. Live."

It takes a great deal of practice and focus—more letting go than focus—because to be present you must let go of this [points to the head/mind]. Let go of your awareness of even what is happening around you and just be still and silent. Still and silent: one of the most powerful healing techniques available. Many humans will say, "Well, I ride my bicycle for my meditation." or "I do some craft." or something. And while that is a form of meditation, it is not stillness: still, silent meditation where you can tap into more than your mind can even conceive. And that is another important thing to note: *what is it* you are tapping into? Because if you can let go of the need to understand, you will receive even more—in the form of knowings, in the form of intuition, in the form of guidance—which is not necessarily words that you hear or pictures that you see. Sometimes it is simply a knowing of what you are to do next. Still silence: a powerful tool for self-awareness, for psychic ability, for evolution.

If you had any idea of how magnificent you are, how perfect your Soul—inside of you and inside every cell and every subatomic particle of you—if you had any idea that the spark that fuels every subatomic particle of you is the Source Itself . . . does that blow your mind? I hope it does. Because if you *knew* that, you would never worry, you would never fear. You would never worry about the future/have concerns about the future. You would allow the future to unfold in your state of *present allowing*. You would no longer worry about the past, because you would realize it is only a concept in your mind. The past does not exist as true reality anymore. If you could see the biggest picture, you would see that it is all energy particles and nothing more—energy particles suspended in a concept of "chair", of "body"—and knowing that you can manipulate the particles easily. But you must believe this is true, you must *know* it. Entertain these ideas for a while and see what happens. Try some *presence* for a moment and see what happens. Try some allowing and accepting of what *is*.

Still Silence

Meditation is a practice. There is no goal. The goal is to do it everyday, to practice, to see what occurs or doesn't occur. To practice, the body and the mind must become still and silent. This is written by other masters, being still and silent. It is said, "Be still and know that I Am God." Say that to your Self: "Be still and know that I Am Source energy."—what some of you call God.

You see Source energy in others, you see it in children, in animals. You see it in smaller animals that have no idea how adorable they are, or at least you think they are. You perceive them as "cute" or "adorable." They don't know. Perhaps they can feel your perception, but not usually. You see the Light there. You see the Light in the mirror. It's very important that you see it there more so than anywhere else. More so than in a piece of art, or a person, or in a leader, or in an icon. Because if you have icons, whether they are celebrities, saints . . . they could see the Light within themselves. That's why you can see it too. When you see it in your Self, others will see it too. Because if you can see it in your Self, then you know you are worthy of all of the abundance that you can handle, all of the Love that you can handle; and then you will inspire others to align themselves in that manner as well.

I, Buddha, am simply a teacher. One who mastered presence. Not at first—it took me some time. But I was able to stay there more and more. And yet, humans thought I was some kind of messiah or something. No. I just took control over my mind. And I mastered that which is available to every individual. That's all. I used the power

that I had within me, just like you have. Everyone has the same power. Everyone has the same opportunity.
***

Presence Meditation

Sit comfortably, relax and take a few deep breaths. Practice presence utilizing the following visualization for the amount of time that you feel is appropriate, and allow Buddha to bless you with the frequency of Love.

So focus on you in this moment. Perhaps close your eyes and take your Self inward. Where do you believe that core spark of Love exists? Is it within your heart center? Is it within the center of your brain? Is it outside of you, surrounding you? Where is it? Notice where you believe it is, because wherever you believe it is, you are correct. But if you do not see it or are not aware of it, then pretend for a moment that it is there. Now, notice its color. Intend that it becomes brighter and engulfs your entire body and energy fields. Expand it to the furthest reaches of your imagination. And now feel its Love. Feel its power. Be present with it.
***

Allowing

In order to be aware of something you must first entertain the concept that it is possible or real, then it will show itself much more easily. So it has been said, "You will see it, when you believe it," and this is true. Believe first then look for the result. But do not be attached to the result—instead be present, open and allowing of the result.

"All of you beautiful, courageous spirits here in physical form right now, we [of the Spirit world] honor you. We honor you for having the courage and doing your best to maintain the energy to stay in this space. These times are more challenging than ever, but you would not be here if you could not handle it. You knew you could, you just wanted to see if you could allow your guidance system to help you remember that you can."

[Radio listener question] All that I had intended to release in my life (people and energies) has been released, and I am now present. What is coming in or what is next?

[Buddha] Excellent. So you are experiencing the side effects of raising your vibrational frequency, and now that you are creating a space for peace (as was mentioned before), it's important to simply be in this frequency now. Be. Just be. And then ask for alignment with your Soul. Start to do some projects. It could be painting, it could be sculpting, it could be graphic design . . . allowing them to come forth in that state of being. It can be dance, it can be singing, some kind of expression; because when you put forth that energetic expression, it attracts to you that same frequency. So what you can expect when you begin to express the Creative Force that wants to come through you, you can expect to attract new people, new opportunities, new situations. Make sure that you continue to sustain the state of being, because you can only attract that which you are.

Notice even the little things that are happening around you, because these are messages also. Notice the behavior of insects and animals, because they are always expressing Creative Force. They are always creating. They are simply flowing through and not thinking. The less you *think*, the more you can *be*. The more aligned you are, the more abundance will continue.

[Radio listener question] "Explain the role of the self-consciousness as it expresses itself through individual personality; the role of self expression as we try to become enlightened and try to become more aligned with the collective consciousness, yet we have our own personalities and expressions of consciousness."

[Buddha] The True Self expresses itself more so through the personality in vibrational frequency than it does with words or behavior. It can be seen through the eyes and can be felt through the heart. This is one way that it is transmitted, and yet it can be transmitted in so many different patterns through the personality, such as dance and art and music and research and writing . . . and yet it is the true state of being that remains from birth until death, regardless of the behaviors that the personality can exhibit.

And so it's not an identity as you think of personality. Sometimes this is difficult to determine from one who is troubled. It is difficult to find that essence, because they have placed around them a shield or armor, so to speak, from negative thinking and from fear. And yet it always remains through the eyes and through the heart. And so it is more important to express your own Self-consciousness than it is to find another's. Because as you express yours, the other one can be given the opportunity—through your energetic expression—to then express theirs. All are spirits in human form.

"Have fun with the one thing you can control—your thoughts."

So think about your perceptions. The one thing *you can control!* Have fun with the one thing you can control—your thoughts. Watch people and events and realities shift, when you shift your perceptions. Play with it! There is no right or wrong way to do this. Just experiment to see if it will work. Many of you experiment to see if you can influence another person's thoughts or actions. What is the judgment behind the desire to change another person's actions or to shift their personality, when they are (in their free will reality) able to choose who they are and how they are expressing themselves from either fear or Love? And you are all expressing your Selves from either fear or Love in any given moment . . . unless you are choosing to be neutral. Most of you cannot sustain that very long—perhaps just seconds—but try it, try it to see. Practice it.

Alignment

So many of your current theories are to think positively to create a positive life. This is very effective. Positive affirmations, positive thoughts, positive choices of perception; these are very effective in order to create a positive outcome. But what of alignment? What of that state where you can have access to so much more? In a positive state you can, of course. But it is the *being* [which aligns]. It is not doing, it is not thinking. It is simply *being* in the moment. And if you spend only five minutes there, you have tapped into Source more rapidly than you can while you are thinking, while you are doing. Meditation is one of the most powerful tools that you can utilize. It costs you nothing except a little bit of time, and it is highly recommended.

Your frequency is a result of how *frequent-ly* you are connecting with Source. Don't think of "What is my frequency?", "What is the number?", "What is my goal?", "Where am I?", "Where do I need to go?", "How do I need to get there?" Just more *frequent-ly* connect. This is what your religions of the world have capitalized upon, actually, because if you are worshiping, so to speak, you're connecting. The more you do this, the more helpful it is to you. This is why religion is helpful for many, because it gives them a structure so that they can take the time to connect and raise the frequency. You can also raise your frequency simply with the intention. I will raise your frequency now.

Pause for a moment, relax and close the eyes, and allow your frequency to rise.

If you just close your eyes and think about alignment, what does this mean to you, alignment? Does it mean that you were praying? Does it mean that you are imagining some connection with your Source or your God? Does this mean that you are peaceful? Calm? You have an inner peace? It could mean all of these things. But what does it mean to *you*? You decide what alignment means to you. And when you do, and when you experience it, you will understand that which everyone is seeking: inner peace, knowing. You will know you have achieved it when you just *know that you know*, and every action that you take is action you know you are meant to take, without analyzing it, without questioning it; and you will know *when you cease asking questions*. Because you'll just know all is

Divine, and all is well in each moment, and all is meant to be, and it is perfect. That's how you'll know when you have arrived. And then when you have arrived at this awareness, see if you can maintain it. You will always be given contrast to challenge you. You are never done here, and that is the beauty of it.

At which frequency do you wish to vibrate now? Or tomorrow? Or five years from now? High vibrational frequency brings with it some interesting experiences, yes? It brings a carelessness which may be perceived as insensitivity. And then your ego mind brings you back to the value of others' opinions—if you may be judged as insensitive—and then you bring your frequency back down and you resonate with the others. No, I am not speaking that you must be different than everyone else—although as you raise your Self, others will raise themselves to match you—it just might be more difficult to do this. It's so much easier to return to a low vibrational frequency that you have once experienced in order to "fit in" or to be part of the "tribe"; but it takes more courage to step away, raising the frequency, not eating junk food, or not engaging in the gossip so that you can rise above duality.

It has been said, and I believe this is important to repeat: that frequency can also be thought of as how *frequent-ly* you are connecting with your Soul or with Spirit; however you define your connection with Source. How frequently are you connecting with Source? How frequently are you re-membering that you are an aspect of Source? How frequently are you making it a priority to let go of things that do not matter, concepts that do not matter, beliefs that do not matter, judgments . . . particularly of your Self? Beating the Self up never helps in any way, in any situation.

Humans gets so wrapped up in their illusion of reality and the responsibilities that they think they must tackle, that they are not taking the time for the connection. It is as though you are not even fueling your Self for your day. You are not even allowing your Self the fuel that you need spiritually in order to go throughout your day while receiving guidance. All humans have the ability to receive guidance all day long, but it is the thinking mind that gets in the way. So what I always recommend is, of course, some kind of meditative practice. It helped me. It helps this one [Cindy]. It helps many people.

Assume that something greater that you cannot imagine— or much more magnificent—shall occur in Divine Order. This concept presented by the Hindu god Vishnu*: "That which is aligned with your Soul's evolution" is a very powerful one for you to adopt or at least experiment with. Asking for *alignment with your Soul's evolution* is a different way of phrasing that you wish to be aligned with your **blueprint**, you wish to be shown that blueprint or guided toward that path. There is not one path on the blueprint. No, there are many paths, many opportunities for detours. And you may choose the detours if you wish, or you may align your Self with the most direct path. There is nothing wrong with choosing a detour, and yet, you will not know if you are doing so unless you are very, very conscious of the way you are feeling and the way you are thinking. You are on a detour when you feel, as you say, "stuck."

**Vishnu Speaks: Messages Of Enlightenment From The Ancient Deity* by Cindy Riggs, p. 15

You're on the pathway that you might call "detour" if you are feeling melancholy, if you are feeling as though you are not moving forward. These are feelings that you have that you are aware of already. So when you are on the path—or the most direct path/pathway in your blueprint—you know this because you feel passion, you feel driven, you feel motivated.

Ask/intend for "this or something I cannot imagine." Because while your brain is magnificent in itself, it does not see the whole picture. It can't see the whole picture. And so you must trust that there is a bigger picture—much bigger—one that expands throughout densities, throughout dimensions, throughout time and space. That picture you cannot see, you must trust that it is there.

Now, there are other times when you are integrating, and this is important to speak of, because this is part of the spiritual growth process. There are integration times when it is time to rest. It is time to simply meditate or to do nothing. There are times when you can't read the materials that you think you ought to be reading. Be gentle with your Self and allow that integration time.

Always know that the Higher Self knows/has all the answers. Sometimes the answers are "no thing"—just peace, just presence—and that is the answer: no action, no thing. And yet sometimes the answer is very different. Sometimes the answer is something that may seem fearful or dangerous, and yet is what the Higher Self needs/wants for its survival, so that it can most authentically *express itself through you* into this space/time/dimension so that others may recognize, others may heal, others may learn. And there is nothing to prove when you are in [**synch**] with the Higher Self/the Soul, because you know that others will understand in the time that is appropriate for their own alignment with their own True Self. But the seeds are planted even from your state of being, your *presence*, your energy pattern. This is why "no thing" is sometimes the most powerful; because if you are in the state of alignment, then others have the opportunity to **entrain** to that state of being as well, without words.

So this one [Cindy] held a newborn child today. She came into synch with it as best she could. What is it that is positive that you can come into synch with? That which does *not* feel like something you want to come into synch with—such as reportings on your news media—step aside, observe without connecting emotion. If you can observe, with neutrality, and assume that it is happening for your benefit/for the benefit of all humanity, then you can rise above very quickly. You can rise above immediately. As soon as you engage in negative emotion, you have lost your Self-control, you have lost your higher frequency. You have to have the Self-control of your mind to choose new perceptions, to choose to engage—or not engage—with certain activities.

What is rampant is the thinking mind. Your thinking minds have gotten out of control. Your egos (as this one [Cindy] calls it) have gotten out of control and you no longer remember how to re-member with your Self. You no longer remember how to connect with the Source of All That Is. You no longer remember how to connect with nature even, in order to receive the messages. It is said that "there may not be wi-fi in the forest," but you still have a connection—an even better connection. And so work on re-membering your Self with the connection with Source—whatever you call this Source of yours: God/Creator/All That Is/**Oneness** . . . do something to connect.

***

Alignment Exercise

Sit comfortably, relax and take a few deep breaths, then take a few moments to connect to Source or Buddha, or any other aspect(s) of Source with the intention of alignment with your Soul's evolution or blueprint. You may even pray/request in this manner: "Thank you for aligning me with my Soul's evolution."

Receive. Allow. Intend for alignment. Be present, and trust, because we of the spirit world only want to assist you along your evolutionary path.
***

Grounding

Remember that Earth is a living being of which you are a limb. It has provided your body here. You are an extension of Earth as well as an extension of Source. And so you, this bridge, must be connected with Source and must be connected with Earth at the same time for the optimum harmony, the optimal balance, and the optimum spiritual, evolutionary abundant state of being.
I am recommending more conscious connecting with Earth's core, and you can do this through the foot chakras/the bottoms of the feet. Using the energy of red helps with grounding and with bringing the messages you are receiving into the 3rd dimension. Remember that

connecting with the core of your Earth raises the frequency also. The very center [Earth's core] has access to unlimited Source energy as well. You can imagine roots growing out of the feet deep into the Earth, or you can imagine some kind of energetic connection from Earth into your feet. This balances and populates your **Merkabah** with energy from both resources from where you come [originate] and helps you to more comprehensively receive guidance. So, on your spiritual path do not always think of what is above. Think of what is also below, providing energy to sustain your physical existence. Keep your Self balanced. "As above, so below."

Creative expression; you have many different ways that you can express creative energy. Any medium you choose is appropriate. Just as I am channeling through this one called Cindy, Creative Force wants to channel through you.

And you have heard the phrase before, but we will say it again. Be true to your Self—your True Self/your true essence/your Soul—always taking action—or no action—that *feels* aligned with that true essence. This is what "being true to your Self" means. Yes, there are some things you will be asked to do that do not feel aligned. But you can shift your awareness around it and still complete the task. You can shift your energy with it, through it. What you *do* is of small importance. How you are *being* is of the greatest importance.

Manifesting Reality

Anxiety is a result of the mind pondering the future or the past. Even if it is something positive that you are desiring and you are thinking about it in the future, this can cause anxiety. Why? Because you are attaching your Self to the outcome. You are attaching your Self to the expectation. Now, I do not wish to shatter your concept of this law of attraction/science. It is a science. And it is, for the most part, real in your 3rd dimensional space. Set your goal, state your desire, think about your intention, and then trust that if it is meant for you, or if it is aligned with your blueprint, then it will occur. And if it is not meant for you or aligned with your blueprint, then it will not occur or manifest.

So at this powerful, powerful time on your planet, have you noticed that things are becoming faster, or seem to be faster: time, events, manifestation or messages? Messages always come quickly, however when you are in a **misaligned** state of being, your message comes quicker than ever, doesn't it? This one [Cindy] has noticed if she is thinking something negative, she will bump into a wall or stub her toe—a message that she is misaligned in that moment. Not every what you call *negative* occurrence is due to your misalignment. Sometimes it is an event that is meant to happen in order to teach you something, propel you forward, give you an opportunity to rise above. All events are opportunities. Some are a result of your misaligned energy, some are not. Some are Divine **gifts** to you from Source/from the **Universe**/from the Oneness—helping you; just as you spank your child to teach him a lesson. Sometimes you need a more dramatic message.

I will also repeat some messages that have been shared before about current state of society, governments. What if everything that is occurring now is also a gift? Because it is. So many people think it is impossible to perceive it in this way. But if you can, you will rise above very quickly.

Everything is energy. And you can either entrain your Self with it, which means come into synch or into the frequency with it, or you can stand outside and observe instead.

Frequency is the state of being that you are vibrating. And you are attracting what you are vibrating. If you're thinking negatively, you are attracting negative experience. And you want a higher vibrational frequency, because at a higher vibrational frequency you are much more peaceful and calm, and you can easily receive your intuitive guidance.

Do not fear that which you are intending to attract. It is no different than one who says, "I have always tended to attract the wrong kind of person as a partner." This pattern of belief will continue to attract that type of partner because there is fear. Once the fear is released, a different type of partner will be attracted. Why? Because when fear exists inside the person, or in the mental and emotional bodies outside the body, it is broadcasting a frequency. And that frequency attracts *like frequency*. It is the same with money. It is the same with anything that you desire. Desire alignment with your Soul. Desire connection with Source. If not Source Itself, request/allow it to be a high-level being, such as myself, a master, a saint or an **Archangel**.

"Go forth and trust that you have more support than you can even imagine, more support than you are aware of. Command our support—with confidence."

The Source of Guidance

You receive inspiration. Inspiration comes from all of us, but primarily from you—the highest part of your Self—

your **Divine Self**. And yet we are all one, so it could be said that it comes from you, it could be said that it comes from any one of us, or all of us. The truth is all of the above. We can't *not* be related. And when one has awareness that you are part of the Oneness, then you begin to open up much more awareness than one who does not have that concept or understanding. You are helping others who are awakening even if you do not speak to them about it. You're helping them simply by *being* how you are. Words and feelings will come and you may be surprised that you "thought" of them, and yet your mind didn't think of those words.

It has been said dozens and dozens of times through this one [Cindy], and I will repeat it because it is so very powerful. If you will intend to align with that Divine spark within you, there is nothing else to be concerned about. Make that your daily prayer/your daily intention. If you align with it or entrain with it, come into synch with it, there are fewer things you need to figure out, fewer things you need to be concerned about, and certainly decisions become effortless. Much of that which is aligned in your environment becomes effortless, because when you are aligned with your Divine Spark/Soul/Divine Self/Higher Self/True Self/True Essence/Divine Essence/Love/Light, then you easily know its guidance, you are operating from within. This is enlightenment.

Believe in your Self. You have heard this before and I will tell you again: you are all-powerful, all knowing, and all wise. There is nothing you cannot conquer, improve, release, create. Go forward and turn illusion into reality—or turn reality into illusion—your choice.

Cycles

Cycles ... everyone is in a cycle, one or more cycles: physically, emotionally, spiritually. You are connected to your planet Earth. You cannot help but be attached to its cycles, but at the same time there are mental cycles occurring, there are emotional cycles, and there are spiritual cycles. So much to keep track of! How is it that you can even go to your job or your school each day and you have all of this energetic stuff to keep track of? Fortunately, it is not that prominent in your consciousness so that it is not that distracting, so that you can stay in the dream and play within it and act within it and choose within it. But this dream is very real as you know. You can feel it. You can feel pain and all of those other labels you have, which are fear-based. You can see, you can touch, you can taste, hear, smell; all of these different frequencies giving you information. You want to see how powerful you are, how confident you are.

How do you know which cycle you're in and what to do? This could take more than your lifetime to describe. And this is why it is important for you to *feel* your way through your reality here. *Feel* it. You have six senses. Feel. It is a *knowing*, it is not touching with your hands, that's touching. It is feeling with your heart, feeling with your gut, feeling with any of your **chakra** centers: your throat, your third eye, your lower chakras, above your head. You can sense things with each one of the centers and with all of the minor chakras that populate your physical body, the bottoms of your feet, your palms. They're everywhere.

So, what cycle are you in? Everyone is in a particular cycle ... a pattern of frequency that you are attempting to hold at this time or to keep fast . . . to keep steady, this pattern. Because it is a new level of comfort you have discovered. It is a new level of awareness and you feel comfortable there and you wish to maintain it. And you do this for a while, however long you choose, until some new information is presented or some new frequencies from . . . oh, say, beings inhabiting the human [Cindy] speaking to you, perhaps? And then this helps to move you to the next level, a new cycle where you work to maintain that frequency for some time. But many of you say you feel "stuck/blocked." It is not that there is a block necessarily, but perhaps you have become too comfortable in your pattern of frequency or your cycle. It is time to spiral into a new one; that is all. Change things up. Do something different to your routine. Something. Anything.

This is why people change their hairstyle and change their clothing, because they want to move into a new cycle. Perhaps they do this every day. You have seen the ones who wear the same clothes every day and there's nothing wrong with that. They are feeling comfortable in the cycle they are in. But if they're longing for *more,* then it is time to change, to allow change to occur. It is not as though you need to make change happen, it is more about *allowing* it to occur, because change always wants to occur for you in some minute fashion.

When you are feeling down, perhaps it is just time for a new cycle to begin or perhaps you are just resisting a new cycle beginning. "I'm depressed," someone will say. Well, first of all you're not *depressed*. You are an eternal spirit. You're not depressed. Depressed is a label for a different statement. When you say, "I am depressed," you are saying, "I am choosing to resist what *is*. I am choosing to resist my guidance. I am choosing to feel bad about something that happened in the past." You're not depressed. You are an eternal spirit with no labels. You are not your personality or your physical body, and yet these things you carry with you, as you hold your patterns of cycles.

The issue of Self-doubt is what I would define as your biggest block. And so if you can let go of doubt—rather, replace it with confidence, remembering that confidence is just a choice, and once you choose it repeatedly, then it becomes part of you—then you will be no longer concerned where your spiritual path is *taking you*. You will be more present with it, and you will be excited to see where it does take you, trusting that it is taking you somewhere. And it may be taking you multiple places. Guiding you to places you cannot even imagine yet.

What you have yet to master is that which you will be helping others to master. Release your Self-doubt and trust your path as though it is a daily discovery. Make it a daily discovery. Simply create the space for peace, as has been mentioned, and then wait to see what happens. See what synchronicities happen in your reality. Wait to see what messages you are given by people or by your social media. Wait to see what numbers repeat in your environment or what song comes on the radio to give you a message. All of these ways that you are being guided are taking you along the path. As was mentioned before, it is not that you are to know where it is taking you now; you are to trust it to take you there without fear.

"You are in a major cycle of the planet and within that cycle you have your own emotional, physical, mental and spiritual cycles occurring. To merge all of these cycles into one, to harmonize the cycles, to align all of them so that you feel very balanced, very secure, very confident, you need only be present and focus on your heart center. You have heard this so many times before, but until you are living it in every moment, we [spirits] will continue to repeat it."

Your Purpose

You want to understand your spiritual path or growth, and the problem here is that you are trying to understand with the mind something that can only be experienced with the heart. And so, when you are trying to understand it, what does this mean? You are trying to define it? You are trying to understand where it is taking you? Or what you are to do with it?

You are here to evolve and to help others evolve. *This is your purpose!* And you do that in the many ways that you choose. Choose ways that are of the highest frequency possible. I will explain.

The ways that you choose to express your Self in the world, whether it is for financial income, for community, for preservation, for healing, for teaching . . . however you choose, make sure it is something that allows you to feel "high" almost—passionate, excited, positive, motivated. And when you make those choices, know that you are going to face contrast every time. I was not allowed to face contrast as a child. I was hidden from reality, given only the best of things and of entertainment. But I wanted to know what was out there. I was curious . . . because minds are curious. And so I left. I left to discover what others were experiencing, and it was very, very difficult to see at first.

Your goal in your process of spiritual growth is not to reach a point where you are blissful all the time/happy all the time, because what is the point of duality? Why would you choose to be in a dual space if you do not wish to experience duality? You came here to experience everything, all of the emotions, all of the experiences that you could. For how do you know what is happy unless you know what is the opposite of what you call happy? How do you know what is Love unless you know what is the opposite of Love, in a space of duality? When you move beyond the space [of duality], when you leave your body at the end of your lifetime, whenever that occurs, you will be re-integrated into pure Love, which just *is*. It is the Is-ness of the All That Is . . . purity, Light, absolute clarity.

You chose to be here. This is a magical place. You think you want absolute clarity, but as soon as you get there you realize how much possibility is here: how much contrast, how much you can experience and feel. If you felt one thing all the time, you would not be content.

We [spirits] are in the same *building* or we are in the same Universe. We are actually in the same **Multi-verse**. The definition of Universe is that there is only one, and this is not true. There are many, many Universes, all connected; all reflections of/aspects of the one Source. And yet, where is that Source? That Source is in the core of each subatomic particle of each Universe in the Multi-verse.

So you, particles, beautiful particles, why the anxiety? Why the frustration? Why the disappointment, particularly when things have not manifested as you expected? You wonder how do I block it? How did I block that which I was attempting to manifest? What am I doing to block it? What am I doing to block joy? What am I doing to block the relationship, or the job, or whatever situation it is that you wish to manifest?

And I can see how you block it. Hmmm . . . you each want a different reason or a different label for each block. But there is only one block and it is the mind. The block is—in the example of the disappointment of that which has not manifested as you expected—the block is that you *expected*. Now, is it wrong to expect? Many of you are aware of this "law of attraction" which is very real and which is truth; and yet, it is not complete truth. There is a piece missing from most of your information, and that is that there is a blueprint—a Divine blueprint—running in the background of each one of you. One that you created. One that you are not allowed to see or understand while you are here, because your purpose here . . . drumroll, as you say . . . your purpose here is to discover that blueprint and to allow it to show itself. You love discovery, you love solving mysteries, yes?

And so allow the mystery of your life to unfold. Let go of your expectations. If something has not manifested as you expected, dissect your mind and determine why you had an expectation; why you thought for a moment that your limited brain could have an expectation, when the truth is that there is always a more magnificent outcome to that which you are expecting. So, some humans will say, "This or something better." Yes? You have heard this? "This or something greater." I would recommend using, at least, *greater* rather than *better*. This term "better" has embedded into it its opposite. So "better" means that there is something that is worse, yes?

Everything that you have experienced has prepared you for what is next. And everything that you experience in that situation will prepare you for what is next. Be grateful for every bit of that experience. It is all contributing to the multi-faceted nature, the multi-faceted being that you are.

When you cease to exist in this physical reality, it's done. You cannot go back. Not in the same way, not in the same body. You go back alright (you have many times) to see if you can play the illusion a little bit differently the next time, have a little more fun, have a little more challenge, learn some things, test your Self, test your strength, test your courage, your individuality, your ability to feel secure, see if you can do these things. Like trying a new sport or a new board game or a new computer game. You want to see if you can do it.

Cycles . . . cycles within cycles. That is what is occurring here. Transition between realities. The transition from this reality into the next. The transition from that one into the next one and perhaps transition from one of those into multiple realities at once. More than your brain can grasp.

You Are Contributing to Evolution

Everywhere you travel, every encounter you make, not only may be a fulfillment of your purpose here, or your mission, or the "list of items on the checklist"; you also absorb something and you affect others. Everything is orchestrated and yet free will operates with in that orchestration, within that architecture. And it is a dance, a magnificent dance of energy, of consciousness, of thought, of emotion.

When one receives information and they write it, perhaps on paper or even in a computer, they are bringing the information into the 3rd dimensional space where it can then affect positively, or inspire, all of the collective human consciousness where the human consciousness resides. So even if someone were to journal every day their thoughts or the inspiration they receive from Spirit, it is possibly affecting all humans even if no human ever reads it. They are still affected on an energetic level. Intend that you are receiving [messages] from high-level guidance.

That is why humans are here: to re-member with Source and to bring that Source energy into the space where everyone is evolving.

***

Golden Light Visualization

Sit comfortably, relax and take a few deep breaths, then proceed with the following visualization, which raises the energy frequency and positively affects the evolution of the collective human consciousness:

Practice [visualizing/imagining] bringing golden Light into your heart/the center of your being. If you even do this for five minutes a day, it will raise your frequency.
***

Healing

The truth is that you all want to be heroes or heroines. Do it with inspiration. You can't save another person's life. You can't heal another person. That is a perception, because only the individual can heal themselves. You can certainly facilitate and inspire that healing process to take place, but you can't do it for them, just as I cannot do it for you.

I will transmit some energy to you in a moment. Perhaps you will feel it. Perhaps you will integrate it. Perhaps it will remain in the outskirts of your energy field for later use whenever you are ready. But I can't integrate it for you, because you are in the free will zone. And in the free will zone this means you have the ability to create whatever reality you want. Not specifics, but frequency, energy frequency. Remember that your frequency is a result of how *frequent-ly* you are connecting with Source.

What is it you would like to heal? Is it a physical ailment? Remember anything that is physical in your body—as disease or misalignment—is often a result (if it has, in fact, manifested later in life) of a mental and emotional issue. I would recommend that you ask for healing, or intend for healing of what you call the "core" issue of that which has manifested physically or the issue of origin that may be holding you back. If you were born with a physical issue, that is a whole different lecture about karma. But know that you chose it. Be grateful for it. Thank it for its gift of teaching, of experience, of contrast.

Do not think only of physical healing. Think also of mental and emotional healing. The solar plexus center is associated with your Self worth, your Self Love, your Self confidence.

Perhaps you think of Self Love in the heart center, and that is true also. But the solar plexus is your area of your identity with your Self. What is your Self? Do you think about what your Self is on a daily basis? Do you think of your Self as your personality? Your physical body? Or do you think of your Self as your Soul or your Spirit? Do you think of your Self as a Soul that has existed in many different expressions or lifetimes? Do you think of your Soul as omnipotent, eternal? Good, because this is all true.

It is important that you understand that healing comes in many forms—not always the form that you expect. Be gentle with your process, allow your Self to heal in your own time—whatever "healing" means to you. And expect that healing may mean something you can't even imagine yet. Remember that your mind only knows what it has been programmed so far to understand. It does not know what is possible. Open yours Self up to possibilities, entertain crazy ideas, or better yet ask your Soul/Higher Self to show you what else is possible.

What else is possible for you to experience here?

Letting Go *Is* Healing

I wish to speak to you of letting go. We [spirits] often speak of letting go and that is truly what healing is. And yet, there is nothing to let go of except expectations and negative perceptions. Because everything that has occurred, everything I have spoken of that contributes to your multi-faceted nature is a "blessing." Remember Divine Order? So it is not that you need to let go of situations or memories or experiences; only to let go of the negative [emotional] charge associated to or assigned to them.

The easiest way to let go is to embrace. Embracing [accepting] the situation. It is not even necessary to understand the lessons, because the part of you that understands the lesson has already integrated it, has already digested it. It is the mind that is last to understand. And when one lets go of the mind, one frees one's Self for unlimited potential, unlimited opportunity, unlimited awareness and knowledge, wisdom and understanding. Understanding not in the mind; understanding in the knowing center, the heart. The knowing center is populated by Love, fueled by Love. Fueled by Truth. Truth is rarely found in the mind, and yet it is understood later in the mind.

Letting go is opportunity for opening of the heart center, more vulnerability. Allow your Self to open up to be vulnerable again. Allow your Self to experience . . . *feel* your reality, *feel* your relationships, *feel* your situations and your decisions rather than think them. And this feeling takes place in the heart center. More opening . . . letting go of the fears of being hurt or being taken advantage of. As you become stronger (higher in frequency), it is okay to let some of your guard down now. The heart is where true intuition takes place, where the clearest guidance comes into you. All you need to do is let go of the understanding and start *being*.

If you feel incomplete with something, then it is important to focus until it is complete. So you determine what "completion" means, and then you create the structure to support that completion; letting go in your own way. You will know when completion has taken place because no more negative thought or emotion will surround the person, issue or event in your memory.

In a moment, you will be receiving the highest frequencies of energy —the highest patterns of frequency—that you are able to receive. I will customize the frequencies based on your intentions. Begin to think of your intentions now. I facilitate your healing, your evolution. And I do intend to align you, perfectly, even for just a moment, so that you will know what it feels like. Because once you have experienced something, you know that it can be experienced again. You can regenerate that experience. My intention is to bring you to pure Love for a short time; no ego, no fear, no apprehension, no anxiety, no guilt. My intention is to raise your frequency so high that those things are absent for a time. That state of being allows healing to take place.

***

Healing Energy Transmission

Sit comfortably, relax and take a few deep breaths, then proceed to allow your Self to accept and integrate the powerful, supportive healing energy transmitted to you from The Buddha. You may even pray/request in this manner: "Thank you, Buddha, for sending me healing energy now. I intend to let go of that which is no longer needed and align with my Soul's evolution."

I am activating your chakras for you beginning with the solar plexus region just below the rib cage and above the navel center. Your navel is the very center of your being. The solar plexus I activate for you is the color

yellow or gold. What does it mean, "activate?" It means that I am allowing some high-level frequencies of energy to penetrate this solar plexus region for you. I am sending it into you so it will activate, or open the center and it will populate that center with more Light, more energy. As I have already mentioned, this helps with Self Love and the healing process.

I will then raise your frequency all over, so that healing can take place. Healing takes place within the will of the person and so I cannot literally heal anyone, but I can provide the energy for healing to take place. So where there are greater deficits of energy, or where there are collections of more negative energy—as you would call it, unnecessary energies—that is where you may see/imagine colors occurring, physical sensations, tingling or vibrations as the higher frequencies enter an area and a shift/change takes place.
***

Buddha Nature/Enlightenment

"I was a rebel! I truly wanted to know the gamut of emotions. I wanted to know the experiences of those on the outside. And I did get to know the deliciousness of suffering, for from it is born: joy, bliss, a higher state of frequency, evolution."

I am called "The Buddha." "Buddha" is a nature. It is a state of being. Perhaps you call this "zen." It is not a state of thinking. But thinking can help you to get there. Thinking can help you intend for that state of being and manifest it. But it is the *no thinking* that actually brings you to that state. The *no thinking*. How do you not think? First of all, you eliminate "how." And then you choose to not think, just for a moment. To *be*, where your mind need not to be anywhere else. When you can do this for a few moments you will slow down time. And when you can do it for a few more moments it will be amazing what you will accomplish in a peaceful way, in a short amount of time. Some of you have experienced this already. Fascinating, isn't it?

Much is misunderstood about my nature. I do not wish to be worshiped. It was never meant for me to be worshiped. "Worship" sounds too much like "war ship." Too much force, too much anxiety, and also too many expectations. Simply intend to become awakened, enlightened.

Each of you has a "Buddha" nature, in that you are programmed to evolve to your Self, programmed to move your Self closer to Source, programmed to take the necessary steps toward enlightenment. But what does this mean? Enlightenment is not one thing that happens overnight. If it were, it would be too overwhelming for you. Enlightenment is something that happens step by step. "Baby steps" is your terminology. One step at a time, similar to a **kundalini** awakening in which the kundalini energy—or the coiled energy at the base of the spine—begins to move itself up the spine; and you see this as a serpent, and yet it is not solid. It is not like a temperature gauge. It is particles that occur. So some particles could reach the crown the first time. Other particles, or the majority of particles, only reaching to the sacral [chakra]. It happens incrementally over time. It is always happening to you. It has been happening. It will continue to happen if you allow it. *Know* you are *allowing* it.

Remember your "Buddha nature." Remember who I am within you, the one who was eternally curious. The one who still is curious. And yet, I knew the questions would be answered in the correct timing. I knew the solutions would come when they were meant to. I knew there was a force outside of me that had all the answers. I knew that some of the answers were inside of me, but I did not know how to extract them. But it didn't matter. I knew it didn't matter, because what most people don't know about me and my life as a human is that I had a different concept of time than others. I never had as much structure as others as a child, even though it seemed as though I had much structure. And yet from my state of *being* there was no structure. Everything around me was structure: my clothing, my meals, my appearances. But everything inside—my creativity, my imagination—was unstructured. And yet the structure was necessary.

I had teachers, many, many learnings—learnings of knowledge, not wisdom. Wisdom comes in the form of creativity, wisdom is found in imagination. Or it could be said that imagination is the vehicle that leads to wisdom. Knowledge is simply collecting data and re-communicating that data, and it is also very valuable. Had I not had the data I was taught, I may not have been able to survive when I went out on my own, following my curiosity, which was stronger than my thirst for knowledge. And I am still curious even now, because there is much, much more to experience in the Universe than I have even experienced yet.

So always be curious. Always seek to understand things more deeply, more multi-dimensionally, from different angles, from others' perspectives; because all perspectives are Divine. All are relevant, valid, and perfect. And this you can begin to translate into conceptual graphic art, into poetry or other prose, to help awaken others who do not have this ability to perceive yet. Because it is this ability to perceive that helps you move forward from this lifetime into other realms. This is why so many repeat [reincarnate]. They have not yet collected the experience. They have not yet allowed the creative imagination to flow through them into the world, making that connection. And as any creative flow is shared—in any form whatsoever—it all becomes part of the human design moving forward. It becomes part of the cellular memory, that which is recorded and stored in the planet and in humans. The path is not me. The path is the path that I discovered: the way of "Buddha" [enlightenment]. It is letting go of structure, letting go of judgment, letting go of what others intend you to be, being a rebel. I was a rebel! I truly wanted to know the gamut of emotions. I wanted to know the experiences of those on the outside. And I did get to know the deliciousness of suffering, for from it is born: joy, bliss, a higher state of frequency, evolution.

You have an enlightened one within you and it is your True Self/True Essence. Connect with it, merge with it, talk with it. Ask it to become more of you, to become more of every moment. Your simple awareness of it/your acknowledgment of it makes it stronger. Every time it is acknowledged it is stronger. This is the part of my Self I had to get in touch with to become enlightened. This is the part of my Self I had to be in touch with in order to handle difficult situations. And they were difficult. I made it so. I created difficult situations for my Self, *consciously*. Most humans now do not choose this consciously. They run from difficulties. So the **subconscious** has to choose the difficulties/conflicts in order to promote growth, promote evolution, promote that merging/connection to Source—through the True Self/the Soul.

When you are aligned with your Divine Spark/Soul/Divine Self/Higher Self/True Self/True Essence/Divine Essence/Love/Light, then you easily *know* its guidance, you are operating from within. This is enlightenment. May you have more and more glimpses of it before the end of your calendar year this year, and even more in your next year. Realize that that which was available to me and to other masters is available to everyone. So don't wait until you have arrived at a certain point or certain goal. Assume you are already there, because part of you *is* already there.

Because I am the "Enlightenened One," I can see far beyond what you can see, and what I can see is the potential within each of you for the enlightenment that I experienced in my lifetime; as well as the enlightenment that is possible beyond this place. I am still on the path of enlightenment even where I am. So know that it is always a process (maybe not infinitely, but always for now), and do not stress your Self about being finished with it in this lifetime. Let go of that. You do not know what your Soul/Divine spark has planned. You do not know how much evolution it has planned in this lifetime or what is appropriate. Trust It. Your mind *helps* you navigate this holographic reality/3rd dimensional space . . . and *some* of the 4th [dimension] and *some* of the **5th**; but you must let go of the mind in order to navigate *more* of the 4th and the 5th and beyond. The more you let go, the more you receive, and this is enlightenment. *Surrender*.

The Lotus Blooms

There are many who have **ascended** as a result of enlightenment; some who have not yet ascended who are enlightened. Why do you not hear about these enlightened masters here on Earth? You hear about some of them. Because when one is enlightened, they no longer are concerned about anybody knowing about it, talking about it, reporting it . . . because they are at peace. They are awakened. They simply *are* in perfect alignment. The ***lotus*** completely open. No fear. No duality. And the enlightened ones usually quickly leave here when there is nothing more to learn, nothing more to overcome. The perfectly opened *lotus* has no past issues, no regrets, no guilt, no anger, no sadness. It just *is*. Some of you have had glimpses of this state of being; perfect alignment. It is good that you have glimpses and it is also good that you continue to have contrast, because there are many, many levels of enlightenment. It is not just one thing to attain. Many levels of it. You catch a glimpse, you have reached one level; you catch another glimpse three months from now, you have reached another level; until you reach the level where that glimpse is permanent: no more questions, no more issues, nothing more to let go of, not much to even remember about the past, and certainly nothing you will need to ponder about the future.

Do not concern your Self with "How far am I in my enlightenment?", "How far am I in my kundalini awakening?"; for when you reach the point of realization, there will be no more need to measure. There will be no more questions. Enlightenment occurs when there are no more questions.

Illumination

Transcript from a Special Event Channeling, March 4, 2016

Divine aspects of Oneness, it is my honor to be in your Divine presence. I am Siddhartha. I come to speak of illumination. What does illumination mean to you? I will tell you what it means to *me* . . . and what it means to *you*.

Illumination, perhaps, is defined as shedding Light on a situation or even illuminating a dark room. And I would encourage you to think about illumination when you think about your relationships, when you think about your work situations, when you think about any other situations in your life. How can you shed more Light on the situation? Do you ask for help? You can, of course. Do you know that there are trillions and trillions of beings standing by, waiting for you to ask for their assistance? I am one of those trillions of beings. And yet, you are as well—one of those trillions of beings who has the capability of shedding Light, of broadcasting Love and Light into your environment.

So you're in a dark room, how can you illuminate the room? You close your eyes. You imagine that the access to Source energy, or the **Source field** of energy, is in your heart center. Perhaps this is the truth. Your access point to the universal life force, to the Source field—or God, some of you call it—is here in the heart center. Deep in the heart center. Allow that Light to spread through the body, out the hands, out every pore of the body to surround you. This you can do in any situation—a situation that you might label as difficult or challenging, or one that is in need of a solution. You can illuminate your own solutions. I come to empower you. I come to enlighten you and yet you were already born enlightened here, just as everyone is. You just forget—on purpose, so that you can see if you remember your way back to the knowing that you are part of the Oneness of All That Is. That spark inside of you is an aspect of Source Itself. So the truth is, even though you are in a physical form here on the planet Earth, in 3rd and 4th dimensions, in a space of duality, in a space of amnesia, the truth is within you. And if you can expand that Light from you, expand that Love force from you, you can shift situations faster than your mind can imagine. You can receive guidance faster than you thought possible. And this is enlightenment.

It is not something to attain from a guru, necessarily, although a guru can certainly help. Many, many teachers can help to plant seeds or to present information that resonates with you and helps you along your path towards Oneness, or your return to Oneness. I am one of those teachers. I have been one of those teachers for thousands of years. And even though I am ascended, even though I am beyond the physical, we are the same. You have access to the same information. All you have to do is remove the mind, quiet the mind, so you can connect and begin to remember.

The energy transmission that I provide for you helps you for this illumination process. I am now going to call this an "illumination initiation" for you. I will transmit *my* energy, which has no ego, which has no personality, and is only pure Love and Light frequencies. If you are confused about Love versus Light, they are the masculine and feminine aspects of creation. Light, the masculine energy, is for knowledge and wisdom, for action. And Love is the feminine Creative Force Itself, that which causes a seed to sprout; that which created the seed to begin with. And you, of course, possess both of these aspects, masculine and feminine, yin and yang, within your Self. These need to be in balance. This is the challenge of the human experience, finding that balance within your Self. So that you can be completely present and receptive to the information that is being broadcast to you, not only from spirits such as my Self, but from your own Soul, your own Divine Self. Which is far beyond the mind. Which is far beyond the one incarnation that you see here now.

So, illumination. If you have the ability to imagine, then you have the ability of illumination. Imagination is your most powerful tool here, because it is that which creates your reality—or at least begins the creation process of your reality. So if you are able to imagine that spark of Light within your heart center, then you can also imagine it expanding. Expanding within you and beyond you.

If you have a plant that is dying, you can simply illuminate it. Perhaps you imagine that you are broadcasting a beam of Light from your heart to the plant, but let go of the expectation, because perhaps the plant has another agenda. Perhaps it is time for it to transition into something else. Because everything is simply energy particles. *Everything*—this chair, the body I inhabit [Cindy's], the body that you inhabit, the carpet that your feet are planted on—all the same particles on the level you call **quantum**. Easy to direct, easy to manipulate. Nothing is held in a pattern here unless you have chosen to believe—or chosen the pattern of belief—that you are holding it in a pattern.

We in the spirit world hear humans all the time say, "It is deeply ingrained.", "This is how I've always been." or

"This is how I was taught as a child." And those are simply concepts you are choosing to hold onto so you can feel safe. So you can have a sense of reference for your Self, a sense of definition/personality. And all of that is illusion. And yet it seems so real while you are here. But I encourage you to play with changing some of those patterns, so that you can watch not only your Self change in a positive way, but things around you become easier, smoother.

Thank you for allowing me to provide not only messages and assistance for you, but also the illumination initiation. This is my way of illuminating you with my frequency. And after I do, you will always hold some of my imprint in your field. You will always be blessed by me, Siddhartha. So you see, I continue to serve even though I am no longer on the planet. Just as many of you will. Many of you Light workers will continue to serve after you transition from here. Many of you already have done so multiple times. Some of you will become spirit guides, perhaps. Some of you will create new patterns of frequency. As humans evolve, new frequency patterns need to be introduced to support that evolutionary process. And that is all this is, an evolutionary process.

I am evolving where I am still, on my journey back toward Source. And yet the Oneness of All That Is, is much more clear to me where I am. It is not as clear to you. And this is why I wish to illuminate you. Just adopt some of these ideas. Entertain them in your mind for awhile. Everyone speaks their truth. I am speaking my truth from my perspective. Other beings of the Universe may speak a truth very similar, but from a different perspective so that you may understand differently. There are many ways to understand the one truth, that is, many different angles.

This is why Source Itself has distributed Itself into all of you, all of us, so that It can experience individual perceptions. So that It can learn new ways of evolving, learn new ways of rising above, and illuminating situations that seem difficult.

But remember that "difficult," "challenge," "frustration," and "good and bad," "right and wrong"—these things are all simply concepts. Everything just *is*. And you have the free will to choose how you perceive that which *is*. The truth is you are an eternal Soul that has no personality or physical body, that has no thoughts. You are beyond thought. You are beyond the need to think, to do, or to create a personality. Remember that part of you. *That* is the spark within you. But you must remind your Self of these concepts each day, until it becomes more and more your truth, your reality. What if this does not resonate with you? Then it does not. Whatever your truth is—is your truth, but if there is any aspect of your life that is uncomfortable, that is unpleasant, then something in the mind is blocking the truth from illuminating you. The mind is usually blocking the Self from receiving Source energy, pure Love.

And if it is not yet quite understood, the seeds have been planted. If, when I illuminate you/initiate you, you feel nothing, do not think you have received nothing. You have received the energy. You *will* receive the energy. Perhaps it will be out in your auric field waiting for you to surrender to it, so it can come closer to you, so that it can integrate with you and become a part of you. And what this does is raise your frequency. And then things are more clear. You can more easily choose to perceive things in a more positive way, in a more loving way. You can choose to see every person as your sister, or your brother, as part of you, as part of me, as part of the entire **Angelic** realm, the creator gods . . . all of us. All one, like a computer network. All connected. All either supporting or inhibiting the other's evolution. So as you support your own evolution, you help to support everyone. And this is truly the most powerful way of contributing or assisting humanity's evolution. To find true Love within the Self, true presence, true connection. And then you, like a virus, spread it through the human collective.

So many ask, "What is my purpose?" Your purpose is to discover what you came here to remember. And if a spirit or human tries to tell you that that is a job title or a specific task, it is not complete. Your purpose usually consists of a list of things. Many tasks. Many objectives. Many experiences. More experiences than objectives, but it *is* for your discovery. Let go of the mind attempting to define it as one path, one thing. And also, humans want to know, "How can I serve?" Serve in whatever way makes you feel joyful, whatever makes you feel loving. And yet, you must be *loving the Self*. So many serve and [use] service as a way to ignore working on the Self or loving the Self. They feel as though, if they are contributing here, helping a person or group, then they are fulfilled. But they are truly not. You must be fulfilled *within* as you serve. You must be full of Light, so that you can share the Light.

As we in the spirit world observe you, more damage is done within the own person's mind than damage done to another person with words or a fist or some other weapon. The most damage we see is the lack of Self Love within the person. First, you must believe you deserve to love your Self. Some do not. They feel fulfilled when they love another and yet it is not true fulfillment. It is mental fulfillment. When you are fulfilled, you feel it in *this* [heart] region of the body, perhaps even in the gut [solar plexus]. You feel such *presence of being* and you have no more questions. You are complete. And then you have even more to share. Some feel tingly as the vibration increases in the physical body and around the body. Some actually see flashes of Light with the eyes closed. Some simply feel lighter, as though the weight has been lifted off the shoulders. Allow that to occur and anything else you are willing to let go of—memories, past hurts—and remember that forgiveness always takes place within the Self. It is always about you, not about the other person. Be as gentle and loving to your Self as you would be to a small puppy or a baby; protecting it, loving it, reassuring it that all is well; sending it Love.

If you are wondering what you need to do to improve your situation, in any aspect of your life, it is not anything you need to *do* at all. It is how you need to *be*. Present and open. If you do not have a meditation practice, there is nothing more powerful with regard to spending your time, if you must have something to *do*. Each time you are in a meditative state, you are more *frequently* connecting with the Source that is deep within you and the *frequency* naturally rises. Conflict, as you call it, will always occur here, to encourage you to rise even higher in frequency. And eventually, you won't even choose to judge it as conflict. You will simply see that it *is*. And you will accept that it is a gift, as everything is here.

So, illumination. I will begin by priming you for what is to come. It is impossible for you to become terribly overwhelmed by your initiation, because you will only receive the amount that you allow your Self to receive.

I am eager for the opportunity to initiate you. This we will begin in a moment as I now finalize the primer energy. Continue now to decide what you are willing to let go of, what beliefs about your Self are you willing to let go of. All of those "I am" statements that you have in you that are not true. Anything that you believe you are not able to do, or is not possible for you. The truth is, you are more expansive than you will ever know, more multidimensional. There are more possibilities in even this incarnation than your mind can possibly conceive. So open your Self up to those *possibilities* and as you illuminate your Self and your environment, those begin to show themselves magically, **synchronistically**.

***

Illumination Initiation

Sit comfortably, relax and allow the Illumination Initiation to take place now. Allow as much time as you feel is appropriate, and notice any sensations or mind's eye images you experience.

Imagine that your body is a sponge. Your whole auric field is a sponge and you are opening the pores, allowing the energy to be soaked in. Soaked into the energy around you, soaked into the physical body. It is pure Love. This is all I give you; illumination and pure Love, because Love is the most powerful weapon for any situation. And that includes, especially, your Self.

***

Once you have received your initiation, it is not complete. I may say that the initiation itself is complete, but you will continue to integrate this for days, weeks, months, maybe even years. The integration pose in Sanskrit is called **shavasana.** So you will lie on your back with your palms facing upward for 15-20 minutes later today/tonight, if you can. Or you can simply sit in your chair with the palms facing up, and this will assist in bringing even more of this closer to you.

You are all one. You are not separate. The more you think of your Selves as one unit, the easier it is to accept others' behavior, the easier it is to heal your Self and others, or at least facilitate wholeness. Healing is about wholeness. Not about what your mind thinks it may be. Wholeness is found when you are merged completely with the Soul part of your Self, when you are connected to the Source of All That Is, and you are in a complete state of loving your Self and others. Illuminate your Self and others. Illuminate your Self in every situation. Throw some Light on your decision-making, on that which is confusing to you, and it will become more clear. Trust and *know* that it will become more clear. You have that power. You have more power than your mind will ever know.

It has been my absolute honor to be in your Divine presence, to share this information, to help you remember that which you already possess, that which you already know is true within you. Each and every day allow this energy to help you to remember more and more the truth of who you are. Divine, eternal, pure Love.

I am Siddhartha.
Namasté ॐ

Glossary

3rd dimension: the space/time reality in which incarnate humans exist; matter, solidity. Also referred to as holographic reality.

4th dimension: also known as the astral plane; a dimension that contains **duality**, occupies the same space as the **3rd dimension**, and is of a higher **frequency**. Existing in the 4th dimension are **spirit** beings and of various **frequencies** such as **spirit guides, spirits** of the nature kingdom and some extraterrestrials.

5th dimension: in Cindy's experience, the 5th dimension is a plane of a higher **frequency** than the **4th dimension**, and is without **duality**. Existing in the 5th dimension are higher-level **spirit** beings such as **Angels, Archangels, spirit guides** extraterrestrials.

All That Is: all aspects of **Source**/Creator/God/**Divine/Creative Force/All That Is/Oneness**; matter and antimatter; quantum **particles**.

Angelic: describes Angels; high frequency **spirit** beings/consciousnesses who have not previously incarnated in human form.

Archangel(s): high frequency spirit beings/consciousnesses who have not previously incarnated in human form and exist in higher realms such as the **5th dimension**.

ascended: spirit consciousness beyond the physical/**3rd dimension** existing at a higher **vibrational frequency**.

aura: also auric field; the energy field that surrounds and emanates from a living being.

blueprint: refers to the **Soul** contract or objectives of the **Higher Self** prior to the human incarnation.

chakra: (Sanskrit: wheel) any of several points or vortices of physical or spiritual energy in the human body according to yoga philosophy. The 7 major chakras are defined below:

> **Crown Chakra** (Sanskrit: Sahasrara) located on top of the head, it is associated with the mind, intellect and perception, and is the connection to the **Divine**; vibrates to the frequency of the color violet and the B tone.
>
> **Third Eye Chakra** or Brow Chakra (Sanskrit: Ajna) located between the eyebrows, it is associated with originality, knowledge, wisdom, intuition, insight, imagination, and mind's eye visions; vibrates to the frequency of the color indigo and the A tone.
>
> **Throat Chakra** (Sanskrit: Vishudha) located between the chin and the top of the sternum, it is the source of sound and controls communication, creative expression, and self-expression; vibrates to the frequency of the color blue and the G tone.
>
> **Heart Chakra** (Sanskrit: Anahata) located at center of the chest, it is associated with emotions like compassion, hope, love, and self-love; vibrates to the frequency of the color green and the F tone.

Solar Plexus Chakra (Sanskrit: Manipura) located at center of the chest, it is associated with emotions like compassion, hope, love, and self-love; vibrates to the frequency of the color yellow and the E tone.

Sacral Chakra (Sanskrit: Svadhisthana) located in the lower abdomen, it is associated with desire, love, passion, sexuality, creativity, inspiration, and connecting with others; vibrates to the frequency of the color orange and the D tone.

Root Chakra or Base Chakra (Sanskrit: Muladhara) located at the base of the spine, it is associated with prosperity and personal safety. It is the foundation for the material world and connection with Earth and instinct; vibrates to the frequency of the color red and the C tone.

compassion: concern for the sufferings or misfortunes of others.

contrast: duality; opposing force.

Creative Force: Source/Creator/God/**Divine/All That Is/Oneness.**

dis-ease: a state of being that is not at ease; disease or illness at its most fundamental, energetic level. See **misaligned**.

Divine: relating to or coming from God or a god; excellent. See **All That Is**, **Creative Force, Oneness, Source.**

Divine Order: the concept or belief that everything is orchestrated; authoritative direction from a higher source of consciousness or collective consciousness. See **Source.**

Divine Self: refers to the direct connection with **Source** and all incarnations; the **Divine** essence which is sometimes used to define a higher **frequency** than the **Higher Self**. See **Soul, True Self.**

duality: the positive and negative nature of human reality in the **3rd and 4th dimensions**; **contrast.**

entrain: the harmonization of an organism to an external **frequency** pattern or rhythm; to resonate with.

evolve: to develop gradually from a simple to a more complex form; to increase vibrational **frequency**.

frequency: the condition of occurring frequently; the number of complete oscillations per second of energy (as sound or electromagnetic radiation) in the form of waves.

gift(s): an unknown or unexpected awareness or occurrence. See **Divine Order**, **karma.**

guidance: also guidance system, guidance team; refers to each individual human's inherent intuitive ability, which may also include **spirit** beings/consciousnesses such as **spirit guides, Angels** or high **frequency** extraterrestrials.

Higher Self: the spiritual aspect/consciousness of a human which is void of personality and individuality; an eternal, omnipotent, conscious, and intelligent being, which is one's **True Self**. See **Divine Self, Soul.**

karma: manifestation of a situation or event as a result of actions in this or previous lifetimes; fate. See **synch**.

kundalini: (Sanskrit: "coiled") the vital energy force lying dormant at the base of the spine until activated by the practice of yoga, which leads one to spiritual awakening, self-realization and transcendent awareness.

Light: spiritual intelligence, knowledge; masculine aspect of **Source**. See **yang**.

lotus: refers to the lotus flower symbol of purity which is popular in Buddhist art and literature, in that the lotus is rooted in muddy waters, yet it rises above, and with many layers of petals it blooms pure and fragrant; also symbolizes enlightenment.

Love: receptivity, creativity; feminine aspect of **Source**. See **yin**.

meridians: energy pathways in the body as described in Chinese medicine and acupuncture.

Merkabah: also Merkaba (Hebrew: Mer = Light, Ka = spirit, Ba = body) the primal pattern or **Divine Light** vehicle that can transport the body from one world to another. A space/time/dimension vehicle of ascension in the form of a star tetrahedron which surrounds the physical body.

misaligned: a physical/mental/emotional imbalance, or state of being which is not true to – or respectful of – the Self or one's inner **guidance**. See **dis-ease**.

Multi-verse: the concept that there is more than one **Universe**.

muscle-testing: holistic kinesiology; a technique used to monitor information about a person's well being.

Oneness: All aspects of **Source**/Creator/God/**Divine/Creative Force/All That Is**; matter and antimatter; quantum **particles.**

particles: the smallest units of energy, according to **quantum** field theory; subatomic.

past life/lives: other incarnations, human or extraterrestrial.

purpose/life purpose: see **blueprint.**

quantum: the **Source field** that contains all subatomic **particles,** according to theoretical physics.

Shavasana: also savasana (Sanskrit: corpse pose) lying on the back with the palms of the hands facing upward.

Siddhartha: Siddhartha Gautama; the birth name of the Buddha.

Soul: the energetic consciousness of a person that is believed to give life to the body and exist eternally. See **Divine Self, Higher Self, spirit, True Self.**

Source: ultimate Creator/God/**Divine Creative Force/All That Is/Oneness**; the origin of all things and no-thing/space. See **yang, yin.**

Source field: the **quantum** field; the origin and location of subatomic **particles**. See **Source**.

spirit: unseen consciousness/force within a person that is believed to give the body life, energy, and power; also refers to the spirit world/realm. See **4th dimension, 5th dimension.**

spirit guides: spirits/spiritual consciousnesses which were previously incarnated as human (in whole or part) who have reached a high level of **frequency** or enlightenment in order to provide assistance to specified or unspecified humans by employing various forms of psychic, energetic communication. In Cindy's experience, spirit guides were once incarnate and often share one or more **past lives** with incarnate humans. See **4th dimension**, **5th dimension**.

subconscious: also unconscious; the innermost self, psyche; the part of the mind that acts and exists without one's conscious awareness.

synch/synchronicities/synchronistically: simultaneous occurrence of events that appear significantly related but without explanation.

True Self: the spiritual aspect/consciousness of a human, void of personality and individuality; an eternal, omnipotent, conscious, and intelligent being. See **Divine Self, Higher Self, Soul.**

Universe: all of space and everything in it including stars, planets and galaxies. Sometimes used to describe **Source**/Creator/God/**Divine Creative Force/All That Is/Oneness**. See **Multi-verse**.

yang: masculine, expressive aspect of **Creative Force/Source**; **Light**.

yin: feminine, receptive aspect of **Creative Force/Source; Love**

About The Author

Cindy Riggs is an internationally known trance channel, psychic, spiritual consultant, educator and public speaker. She is a former TV producer, writer and show host, and has appeared as a guest on numerous radio shows. She has written articles and audio programs, and is also the author of ***Vishnu Speaks: Messages of Enlightenment From The Ancient Deity.***

Cindy has been channeling since 1997, which is the process of exclusively allowing high-level spirit beings to temporarily inhabit her body and energy fields in order to speak and transmit energy through her. Cindy regularly channels for both public and private sessions, events, and has channeled on live television, radio and webstream. Links to radio shows and transcripts from some channeling events are available on CindyRiggs.com.

In her private practice, Cindy performs psychic/spiritual guidance, Defragmenting (soul retrieval), hypnosis, past-life regression, spirit releasement, energy healing, along with personal and psychic development coaching. She is also a Reiki Master/Teacher and Licensed Minister. Cindy also travels and works remotely. Visit her at CindyRiggs.com.

Made in the USA
Middletown, DE
10 July 2016